# The Essential Slow Cooker Recipe Cookbook #2021

## Fast and Nutritious Recipes for The Whole Family incl. Vegan and Vegetarian Bonus

George C. Patterson

ISBN- 9798686804715

# TABLE OF CONTENTS

Whether you're a busy parent who is running around looking after little ones all day or a stressed-out professional who simply lacks the time to prepare nutritious meals after work, a slow cooker could be the ultimate solution. Representing the easiest way to make delicious dishes of all kinds with minimal effort, a slow cooker enables you to enjoy all of your favorites but prepared in the most convenient way.

Never again will you need to slave for hours over a hot stove. With a slow cooker in your kitchen, you can simply throw a few ingredients into the pot, flick a switch and go about your day. When you return home, or when you're ready to eat, you can simply open the lid to the mouth-watering aroma of a freshly prepared dinner which is all ready to serve.

The choice of meals you can prepare in a slow cooker is almost endless. Whether you love meat or poultry casseroles, roasted joints, soups, stews, or even desserts, this trusty kitchen appliance can shoulder the burden for you. No more wasting time stirring pans and juggling baking trays – all you need is a single gadget and this helpful recipe book.

If you're ready to discover the best fast and nutritious recipes for your whole family, all of which can be whipped up in your slow cooker, you've come to the right place. So, read on – you're sure to find something that tickles your taste buds!

# WHAT IS A SLOW COOKER?

A slow cooker is a small electrical kitchen appliance which has been around for over three decades and which is designed around the principle of slow cooking.

So, what does slow cooking mean?

The answer is quite simple. Just put ingredients into a container then allow them to slowly cook until the meal is done. This method can be found in use in pig roasts and barbecue pits where a low temperature paired with lots of time allows the meat to eventually become very tender.

You can slow cook using dry heat, such as in a roaster or oven. Alternatively, you can slow cook with liquid. In a slow cooker, you'll be using moisture in an unusual way since it will remain sealed while the cooking process is underway. When the food cooks, it releases steam. This allows condensation to collect in the device to act as a form of baster.

People have been slow cooking for centuries, but electric slow cookers originally became popular during the 1970s. While they fell out of fashion briefly when the microwave emerged onto the market, they have recently seen a comeback and a demand has arisen for cookbooks like this to help home cooks find tasty one-pot recipes for their families.

The original slow cookers were created based on the electric bean pot which was invented during the 1960s for steeping dry beans. A reworked electric bean pot became the Crock-Pot which allowed cooks to produce a full meal in a single pot. This device took off in a big way since career women of the day were looking for a way to save money and time in the kitchen after a hard day in the office.

Slow cookers feature three key components:

- ◆ The lid
- ◆ The inner container
- ◆ The outer casing

The metal outer casing contains low-watt heating coils which cook the food. These are encapsulated completely by the casing. Meanwhile, the container inside, also known as the crock, is manufactured from ceramic and it fits into the heating element. Many models have removable crocks. Finally, the domed lid will fit tightly on top of the crock.

When you switch on your slow cooker its electric coils warm up, transferring the heat to the gap between the container and base wall from the device's outer casing. The heat will warm up the crock pot to 180 – 300 degrees Fahrenheit. This heating method simmers all the ingredients in the pot for a number of hours at a lower temperature until finally, the food has been thoroughly cooked.

While the food is cooking, it will release steam which gets trapped by the lid. This condensation will create a seal between the crock's rim and its lid. This adds more moisture to your food while also aiding the process of cooking.

Typically, slow cookers have 3 different settings – off, high and low. Some slow cookers are programmable, and in such cases, the device switches onto a warming setting once the food has cooked to ensure your meal can be served at the optimal temperature.

# WHAT ARE THE BENEFITS OF A SLOW COOKER?

Cooking with your slow cooker can save you a lot of time, yet you'll still enjoy a meal that is delicious and nutritious. Just assemble a few ingredients when you get up, put them into your slow cooker, switch it on, then when you return in the evening your dinner will be ready with very little mess and just a few dishes to wash.

Slow cookers only need a little electricity to do their work too when compared with your regular oven. So it'll save you money while also helping to keep your kitchen cooler – something that couldn't be more important if you live in a warm area.

Slow cooker meal preparation is also economically smart since you're able to use a cheaper cut of meat. The condensation produced during cooking bastes the meat so cuts which are traditionally tougher can become tender. Just because you save money and time doesn't mean you'll sacrifice taste. Your meat will be wonderfully succulent while vegetables that are cooked this way absorb spices and stocks to give them a fuller flavor.

Since your slow cooker will have a low and a high setting, you can easily adjust the temperatures to suit the amount of time that you need the dish to cook. While cooking at a low temperature is very safe, it's recommended to cook on a high temperature for the first hour so you can be certain your food has cooked through completely.

# WHAT CAN I COOK IN A SLOW COOKER?

Most people want to cook meat dishes in their slow cooker, however, you need to ensure that frozen meats have been properly thawed before cooking or they will take far too much time to cook through. When you cook meat, you must heat it up to at least 140 degrees Fahrenheit as rapidly as possible so any bacteria can be killed. You must also ensure that the meat's internal temperature is in the range recommended before you serve it.

Poultry also cooks well in a slow cooker, however, when you do this, you should try to use poultry that still has the skin on as this keeps the meat nicely moist during cooking.

Vegetables can also be cooked in your slow cooker, but remember that preparing them to put into the slow cooker is going to take a little longer than preparing meat. Cut vegetables uniformly so that they can evenly cook. Also, vegetables often take longer when it comes to cooking than meat. Therefore, if you're preparing a stew or a meat-and-vegetable dish, make sure the vegetables are layered first on the crock's bottom.

Some popular slow cooker recipes are stews and soups since slow cookers are designed to stay on a simmer at low heat for a long period of time. Just ensure your favorite soup ingredients are covered with water and make sure that any other liquids added during the cooking process are brought up to a boil before adding to the pot so they won't lower the cooking temperature of the meal.

You can even prepare spreads and dips in a slow cooker. The lower heat can keep cheese-based dips warm but won't burn the ingredients. If dips are maintained on a lower heat, the ingredients also won't congeal during your party or dinner.

It's even possible to prepare grains in your slow cooker. Cracked wheat, oatmeal or rice porridge may be cooked during the night so you can rise to a nutritious, hot breakfast. Bread-based dishes and bread can be made in your slow cooker too thanks to the lower heat setting allowing the dough to rise.

One of the most surprising categories of dish to prepare in your slow cooker is desserts. Of course, you can prepare tapioca or rice puddings, but you may be more amazed to discover you can make a cake or hot fruity dessert with ease.

# MAINTENANCE AND SAFETY WHEN USING A SLOW COOKER

A slow cooker is designed for cooking food for a number of hours while heating the food properly. Yet, taking safety precautions is still important.

Here are some tips for maintenance and safety when using your slow cooker.

- Don't fill the container to a level more than 2/3rds full and make sure the lid is kept on during cooking so that the optimal cooking conditions can be maintained in the container.
- Make sure you periodically test your cooker to ensure it is heating up correctly and can cook the food to the right serving temperature. Make sure that food is cooking to a minimum of 140 degrees Fahrenheit within a minimum of 4 hours to ensure it won't harbor bacteria.
- Test the slow cooker by filling it to ½ - 2/3rds with water then use the lid to cover it and cook at the lowest setting for at least 8 hours. When the time has elapsed, take your food thermometer and check the temperature of the water before it has time to cool down. If the reading is over 185 degrees Fahrenheit you can safely use your slow cooker. If the temperature is lower, its heating element may not be working properly and therefore, your food may not be able to cook thoroughly.
- You can safely leave your home while your slow cooker is switched on since it runs on low wattage. While the base will heat up, it won't get excessively hot so there's no danger of fire.
- Don't immerse the slow cooker's base in water. Should your model have no removable container, use a sponge and soapy water to clean its interior then wipe any spills away.

- Extreme temperatures may cause the container to crack. This means you shouldn't use it on your stovetop or in your freezer. Also, don't put the hot crock onto a cold surface or pour any cold water in it.

- Make sure all poultry and meat are thawed thoroughly before you add them to your slow cooker. Before you serve up, use a food thermometer to check that they are hot enough.

- If you're using beans to prepare a recipe, remember dry beans cannot be used in slow cookers. Dry beans contain toxins which may result in vomiting, nausea, abdominal pain and diarrhea. Soaking then boiling your dry beans will remove the toxin so your beans are safe for eating. Slow cookers don't get hot enough so dry beans cannot be heated sufficiently to remove the toxin. This means you need to soak dry beans for at least 12 hours before rinsing them, boiling them for ten minutes and then adding them to the slow cooker. Alternative use a can of beans.

- Slow cookers must only be used for cooking and not for reheating. Store any leftovers in a shallow container and refrigerate them within 2 hours of serving the meal. You should reheat the leftovers in a microwave or on your stovetop, taking care to ensure the temperature reaches 165 degrees Fahrenheit.

# TIPS FOR PERFECT SLOW COOKING

If you want to make sure that your slow cooked meal is perfect every time, follow these expert tips to get the ideal result with every dinner you prepare:

- ◆ Ensure you've always set the appliance to the correct temperature. If you're in a hurry, you might want to choose the higher temperature setting. Should this apply, be aware the cooking time at the high setting is jut more than half of the time taken on the low setting.

- ◆ Ensure your slow cooker has been placed on a steady and sturdy surface. One top tip is to put your appliance onto a towel since this will be able to absorb any possible liquid which spills or spits out. Make sure your cooker doesn't touch other appliances or the wall while it is switched on because of the heat that it produces which may cause damage.

- ◆ If you're using herbs in your meal opt for dry ones rather than fresh whenever you can. This is because fresh herbs go limp and brown in the moist, long cooking process. Meanwhile, dry spices and herbs release their flavor with time.

- ◆ Any leftovers should be taken out of the pot, transferred into a fresh container, allowed to cool then refrigerated and frozen. Never allow the food to get cold when inside the slow cooker since it will retain the heat for a considerable period after the appliance has been switched off and this could all bacteria to build up as the food cools down. This could make you ill if you then go on to eat the contaminated food.

- ◆ It can be tempting to lift up the lid of your slow cooker to check to see how well the cooking process is going. However, if you do, the heat lost will extend the length of time your meal will take to cook considerably. Each time the lid is lifted, you'll be added around half an hour of additional cooking time to your meal, so bear this in mind and avoid taking off the lid.

# HOW DO I MAINTAIN MY SLOW COOKER?

Slow cookers may make mealtimes more convenient and simple but you'll still need to take the time to maintain your appliance properly if you want it to carry on functioning properly. Despite all of the advantages that slow cookers bring, they can become very dirty with caked-on mess from the one-pot dishes you're preparing. It can be hard to remove this mess without damaging the pot, so how can a slow cooker be made clean without causing any problems?

## Read The Manual First!

Before you start to clean your slow cooker, make sure to read the manufacturer's manual first. Not every slow cooker is the same. Some are made from stainless steel, others from aluminum, plastic or even glass. All need to be treated differently. That means checking the manual couldn't be more vital since you might end up invalidating your warranty if you get carried out with using harsh cleaning solutions or removing components that are supposed to remain intact.

## How Do You Clean Slow Cookers?

To clean slow cookers properly you require:
- Dishwashing soap
- White vinegar
- Baking soda
- Ammonia
- A cotton or microfiber cloth
- A scrubbing brush

- ◆ A screwdriver

First, ensure you've unplugged your appliance before you begin cleaning. Wipe the exterior down with a clean, damp cloth as this is a mild way to start cleaning your cooker. You should try this before you move onto a tougher option For many cookers, detergent and warm water will be sufficient to produce a good, clean result. A harsh cleaner may end up damaging the cooker's finish or even causing some damage to its working parts.

If there are stubborn stains stuck to the exterior of the cooker you can remove them by using a mix of water and baking soda. Alternatively, you can opt for a cleaning solution that is designed for use on that particular surface materials such as a cleaner specifically for stainless steel.

Splashes and spills can end up under the appliance too. Wipe beneath it and then use a small brush so any crumbs are removed that are lodged in the open areas.

Nest, clean the container that goes inside the cooker. Soaking the pot in some water and mild detergent may work well, or if you have a dishwasher you may be able to put it in on a regular wash.

If food is stuck to the inside of the container fill it up with water then cook it on a low setting for a few hours. This should help stubborn food to come off easily. Afterward, put it into the dishwasher.

Add some baking soda to water and use it to scrub the container of your slow cooker. This will scour it but won't be too abrasive. For any remaining cooked-on food, fill up the container to its top with water, then add some baking soda along with dishwashing detergent then turn on the appliance to a low heat setting. Afterward, remove the water then wash the container as usual.

A model that is made with dark stoneware may have remaining mineral deposits due to repeated cleaning and use. Sometimes, it just needs a deep clean to bring it back to its original pristine condition Fill up the container with water, then add a cup of white vinegar and allow it to soak thoroughly overnight.

Under the slow cooker's container, you'll find its heating element. Sometimes, food spills into that area and this means its interior casing often needs to have stains removed too. Never submerge the inner casing in water. Also, ensure it's fully cool before you clean it. Since it contains electrical components use only a clean, damp cloth for wiping the interior.

If there are cooked-on, tough stains on its inner casing, you can pour ammonia into a bowl, put the bowl into the cooker then cover it and allow it to rest overnight.

Finally, clean the removable components such as knobs, handles and lids in soapy warm water and use your small brush to remove any lingering particles of food. Once every component is dry, you can reassemble the appliance and it'll be ready to use again!

# Meat And Poultry Slow Cooker Recipes

Most people associate using their slow cooker with preparing meat and poultry stews and casseroles, and indeed, these appliances are great for this. However, there are many other meat-based meals that you can make in these clever gadgets that are sure to surprise you. Read on to discover some of the very best slow cooker recipes involving your carnivore favorites!

# HOMESTYLE CHICKEN CASSEROLE

Combining the smokiness of chorizo with the sweetness of paprika in a wonderfully rich tomato-based sauce, this recipe for chicken casserole is the ideal way to feed your whole family on a cold winter's evening. Since a major component of this recipe is butter beans, all you'll require for serving is some tasty crusty bread to soak up the juices.

*Serves Four*
*Preparation Time: 15 minutes*
*Cooking Time: 3 Hours 15 Minutes*

## NUTRITION PER PORTION:

KCAL – 382

FAT – 9 G

SATURATES – 3 G

CARBS – 30 G

SUGARS – 7 G

FIBER – 6 G

PROTEIN - 41 G

SALT – 0.88 G

## INGREDIENTS:

- 600g//1lb 3oz boneless and skinless fillets of chicken thigh
- 2 tablespoons of olive oil
- 225g//1/2 lb sliced chorizo
- 1 tablespoon sweet smoked paprika
- 2 chopped red onions
- 2 chopped garlic cloves
- Pinch of saffron
- 1 tablespoon of plain/all purpose flour
- 70g//1/4 cup of tomato puree

- 2 stock cubes (chicken) made up with water to 600ml//1 pint of liquid
- 3 sticks of celery chopped into pieces of roughly 3cm each
- 250g//1 ¼ cups baby tomatoes
- 2 cans of butter beans/lima beans, drained and rinsed
- Handful of chopped parsley

## METHOD:

1. Turn on the slow cooker and set it to medium. Next, add the paprika to 1 tablespoon of olive oil and use this mixture to coat the fillets of chicken thigh well. Season well with pepper and salt, then set to one side.

2. Pour 1 tablespoon of olive oil into a frying pan or skillet over a medium to high heat. Add the chopped chorizo and cook for 4 minutes. Turn down the heat to a medium setting, then add the chopped red onions and continue to cook for 4 minutes more.

3. Add the flour and garlic to the pan and cook for 1 minute before removing and setting to one side. Meanwhile, put the pinch of saffron into a heatproof glass and pour 2 tablespoons of boiling water over it to infuse.

4. Take the frying pan or skillet that you used for cooking the onions and chorizo and heat it once more over a medium to high heat. Put the chicken in the pan then brown it on both sides until golden.

5. When this is complete, add the onions, chorizo and chicken to your slow cooker. Add the tomato puree and pour the stock over all of the ingredients. Add the tomatoes, saffron-infused water and celery and stir well. Cover with a lid, then allow to cook for 3 hours.

6. If the chicken is tender after this time, add the lima beans/butter beans and allow to cook for another 15 minutes.

7. Share out the casserole between 4 bowls then top with the chopped parsley. This dish is delicious served with quinoa or couscous, or with slices of fresh crusty bread for dipping.

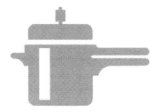

# BEEF AND PRUNES

If you're looking for a delicious yet simple dish to serve up as part of a satisfying Sunday dinner, this slow cooked beef recipe is the ideal choice. Pairing melt-in-the-mouth brisket with the sweetness of prunes, every family member is sure to come back for more.

> *Serves Six*
> *Preparation time: 15 minutes*
> *Cooking time: 4 to 8 hours*

## NUTRITION PER PORTION:

KCAL – 342

FAT – 10 G

SATURATES – 3 G

SUGARS – 16 G

SALT – 0.7 G

CARBS – 20.7 G

PROTEIN - 36.8 G

FIBER – 3.4 G

## INGREDIENTS:

- 900g//1lb 9 oz brisket/braising steak
- 3 tablespoons of olive oil
- 250mls/8 fl oz red wine
- 2 tablespoons of flour
- 2 chopped yellow onions

- 2" piece of chopped peeled ginger
- 2 chopped garlic cloves
- 2 teaspoons of cumin powder
- 250mls/8 fl oz beef stock
- 150g//1 cup of prunes
- 2 tablespoons of honey

☀ 1 red onion                              ☀ A handful of parsley to serve

**METHOD:**

1.  Switch the slow cooker on to heat up. Slice up the brisket or steak into 2" pieces and season them well.

2.  Heat up a tablespoon of olive oil then sear the beef well on every side.

3.  Remove the beef from the frying pan and then set it aside.

4.  Pour the rest of the olive oil into the pan together with the ginger, garlic and onion.

5.  Saute gently for 8 minutes.

6.  Put the flour into the pan and cook for another 2 minutes.

7.  Add the red wine, cumin, prunes, honey and beef stock.

8.  Mix the ingredients together well then put them all in your slow cooker along with the brisket or braising steak.

9.  Put the lid onto the cooker.

10. Cook on a high heat for 4 hours or for 8 hours if you prefer to cook it on a low heat.

11. Serve with mashed potato and with the red onion and parsley sprinkled over it.

# SLOW-COOKED CHILLI CON CARNE

This richly spiced chipotle and beef chilli is ideal for warming up the whole family on a cold Fall evening. Perfect for busy weekends or workday evenings, this delicious and flavorsome dish is perfect served with rice or with cheesy nachos and a dollop of sour cream.

*Serves 6-8 people*
*Preparation time – 25 minutes*
*Cooking Time – 6-8 hours*

## NUTRITION PER PORTION:

KCAL – 281
FAT – 13 G
SATURATES – 4 G
CARBS – 18 G
SUGARS – 7 G
FIBER – 6 G
PROTEIN – 19 G
SALT – 0.03 G

## INGREDIENTS:

- 3 tablespoons of olive oil
- 500g//1lb 20 oz of beef mince
- 2 grated garlic cloves
- 1 chopped onion
- 1 chopped celery stick
- 1 sliced red pepper

- 2 teaspoons of ground cumin
- 2 teaspoons of dried oregano
- 1 teaspoon of smoked paprika
- 3 tablespoons of chilli chipotle paste
- 3 tablespoons of tomato puree

☀ A can of pre-chopped tomatoes     ☀ 4 squares of dark chocolate

☀ 400 ml//13 fl oz of beef stock     ☀ 2 cans of drained black beans

## METHOD:

1. Set your slow cooker onto a low heat and heat half of the olive oil.

2. Fry the beef mince in the oil for 12 minutes then add it to your slow cooker.

3. Warm the rest of the olive oil and fry the celery, pepper and onion in it for 10 minutes until soft.

4. Add the paprika, cumin and garlic and fry well for one minute before adding to your slow cooker.

5. Stir the chipotle paste, oregano, stock, tomatoes and tomato puree into the crock pot's container.

6. Cover with the lid then allow to cook for between 6 and 8 hours.

7. Stir the beans into the mix and add the chocolate in the last half hour of cooking.

8. When ready, serve with rice or nachos and sour cream.

# SLOW COOKED LAMB LEG JOINT

You may never have thought of cooking a roast joint in your slow cooker but it's perfectly possible and this lamb leg joint is the ideal example! The result will be flavorsome, tender and melt-in-the-mouth good. Serve it with steamed vegetables and mashed potatoes for a wonderful Sunday dinner.

*Serves six*
*Preparation time – 15 minutes*
*Cooking time – 8 hours*

### NUTRITION PER PORTION:

KCAL – 356

FAT – 21 G

SATURATES – 9 G

CARBS – 5 G

SUGARS – 1 G

FIBER – 0 G

PROTEIN – 33 G

## INGREDIENTS:

- 2 tablespoons of olive oil
- One tied lamb leg joint
- 1 tablespoon of unsalted butter
- 300mls//10 fl oz lamb stock
- 2 tablespoons of all purpose flour
- 2 sliced red onions
- 2 sliced garlic cloves
- 5 thyme sprigs
- 5 rosemary sprigs

## METHOD:

1. Heat up the olive oil then put the lamb leg into the skillet and brown it well on all sides for 5 minutes. Turn on your slow cooker onto a low heat setting then melt the unsalted butter until it foams. Stir the butter into the flour and whisk the stock into it gradually. Bring it to a boil and set aside.

2. Put the sliced onions, thyme, rosemary and garlic into the slow cooker. Put the lamb leg on top then pour the gravy over it.

3. Put on the lid then cook for 8 hours until tender.

4. Take the lamb out of the slow cooker and put it onto a plate, covering it with aluminum foil.

5. Into a saucepan, strain out the liquid then simmer it until it has become slightly thick.

6. Slice the lamb thickly and serve with green vegetables, gravy and mashed potatoes.

# PULLED CHICKEN COOKED SLOWLY

If you're a fan of pulled pork you're going to love this alternative that can be easily prepared in your trusty slow cooker. Pulled chicken is a little lighter than pulled pork but it's equally delicious and is perfect for sandwiches, burgers and just for eating as it is served with nachos or fries.

*Serves 8 to 10*
*Preparation time – 5 minutes*

## NUTRITION PER PORTION:

KCAL – 398

FAT – 17 G

SATURATES – 4 G

CARBS – 22 G

SUGARS – 19 G

FIBER – 3 G

PROTEIN – 37 G

SALT – 0.7 G

## INGREDIENTS:

- 2 tablespoons of vegetable oil
- 12 skinless and boneless chicken thighs
- 250mls//8 fl oz passata
- 2 sliced and halved red onions
- 2 crushed garlic cloves
- 2 teaspoons of paprika
- 100g//1/2 cup barbecue sauce
- 2 tablespoons of chipotle paste
- 1 tablespoon of brown sugar
- 1 juiced lime

## METHOD:

1. Turn your slow cooker to a low heat then heat up a tablespoon of vegetable oil in your skillet.

2. Brown the boneless chicken thighs, transferring them into your slow cooker.

3. Pour the rest of the oil into the pan.

4. Fry the red onions for 5 minutes until soft.

5. Stir the paprika and garlic into the onions and fry for 1 minute more.

6. Tip everything in the pan into your slow cooker.

7. Pour 100 mls//3 fl oz of water into the pan and swirl it around.

8. Pour the water into your slow cooker.

9. Add the passata, chipotle, lime juice, sugar and barbecue sauce and stir well.

10. Cover with the lid then cook for 6 - 8 hours.

11. Use forks to shred the cooked chicken thighs.

12. Serve in a bun, taco shell, or with rice.

# SLOW COOKED CHICKEN CHASSEUR

This traditional French dish can be prepared quickly and easily in your slow cooker and will melt in the mouth as the ingredients become soft and tender over the course of the day.

> *Serves two*
> *Preparation time – 15 minutes*
> *Cooking time – 6 hours 35 minutes*

## NUTRITION PER PORTION:

KCAL – 486

FAT – 26 G

SATURATES – 6 G

CARBS – 15 G

SUGARS – 12 G

FIBER – 4 G

PROTEIN – 29 G

SALT – 1.4 G

## INGREDIENTS:

- 2 tablespoons of olive oil
- 1 onion or 2 shallots, chopped finely
- 5 bone-in, skin-on chicken thighs
- 200g//1/2 lb halved mushrooms
- 2 crushed garlic cloves
- 200mls//6 ¾ fl oz white wine
- Half a can of chopped tomatoes
- 1 tablespoon of tomato puree
- 2 sprigs of thyme
- A bay leaf
- 400 mls//13 ½ fl oz of chicken stock

## METHOD:

1. Turn on your slow cooker and set it to a low temperature. Pour the olive oil into a skillet and put over a mid to high heat. Put the chicken into the pan and fry it with the skin side facing down for 5 minutes before turning and frying it on the other side for another 4 minutes until the thighs are golden brown all over. Place the thighs onto a plate then set to one side.

2. Put the shallots or onion into the skillet and fry over a mid heat for 10 minutes. Add the mushrooms and garlic and continue to fry for another 10 minutes.

3. Pour the white wine into the skillet and allow to bubble for several minutes until it has reduced.

4. Sir the tomato puree into the pan, along with the herbs and chopped tomatoes then simmer.

5. Pour the prepared sauce into your slow cooker then place the chicken on top in a single layer.

6. Pour the stock over everything to cover the thighs.

7. Cover with the lid and allow to cook for 6 - 8 hours.

8. When the chicken has become tender and the sauce is thick, put the chicken on a plate.

9. Allow the sauce to bubble for another 5 minutes leaving the pot's lid off.

10. Serve the sauce and chicken with mash or pasta.

# SLOW COOKED CHICKEN KORMA

Even those who aren't fans of curry are sure to appreciate this slow cooked chicken korma prepared at home with minimal effort. This is certain to be a great family favorite with its tender chicken served in a fragrant and rich curry sauce that is just mild enough to be ideal for kids.

> *Serves four to six people*
> *Preparation time – 15 minutes*
> *Cooking time – 6 hours and 20 minutes*

## NUTRITION PER PORTION:

KCAL – 511

FAT – 33 G

SATURATES – 11 G

CARBS – 10 G

SUGARS – 8 G

FIBER – 3 G

PROTEIN – 43 G

SALT – 1.4 G

## INGREDIENTS:

- 2 cloves of garlic
- A peeled piece of ginger (around the size of your thumb)
- 2 chopped onions
- 2 tablespoons of vegetable oil
- 2 tablespoons of tomato puree
- 6 chopped chicken breasts without the skin
- 1 teaspoon of ground cumin
- ½ teaspoon of chilli powder
- 1 teaspoon of paprika
- 2 teaspoons of sugar

- 1 teaspoon of turmeric
- 1 teaspoon of ground coriander
- 150 mls//5 fl oz double cream
- 300 mls//10 fl oz chicken stock
- 6 tablespoons of ground almonds

**METHOD:**

1. Turn on your slow cooker and turn it to a low heat setting.

2. Put the onions, ginger and garlic into a blender and add a little water before whizzing into a paste.

3. Warm the oil over a mid-high heat in a skillet then add the chicken and sear it all over.

4. Take the chicken out of the skillet and put it to one side and add the paste from the blender.

5. Fry the paste over a mid-high heat for 10 minutes until it is lightly golden.

6. Stir the spices, tomato puree, sugar, and 1 teaspoon of salt into the skillet and fry it for 1 minute before putting the chicken into the skillet once more and adding the stock.

7. Next, stir well, bringing it to a gentle simmer before spooning everything into your slow cooker.

8. Allow to cook for 5 to 6 hours.

9. Stir the ground almonds and cream through the mix and allow to bubble for 10 minutes in order to reduce.

10. Serve with naan bread and rice.

# SLOW COOKED BEEF GOULASH

This may be a traditional recipe, but when you prepare it in your slow cooker you're sure to be impressed by how tender and delicious the beef, peppers and tomatoes become. This is a rich, creamy stew that is comforting, tasty and sure to please the whole family.

*Serves 8*
*Preparation time – 25 minutes*
*Cooking time – 7 hours*

## NUTRITION PER PORTION:

KCAL – 581

FAT – 32 G

SATURATES – 13 G

CARBS – 17 G

SUGARS – 12 G

FIBER – 6 G

PROTEIN – 54 G

SALT – 0.3 G

## INGREDIENTS:

- 3 tablespoons of olive oil
- 2 chopped onions
- 2 kg//4 lbs 4 oz chunks of stewing steak
- 5 chopped peppers
- 3 crushed garlic cloves

- 2 tablespoons of flour
- 2 teaspoons of caraway seeds
- 1 tablespoon of sweet smoky paprika
- 2 teaspoons of hot smoky paprika
- 4 tablespoons of tomato puree

☀ 500 mls//17 fl oz beef stock     ☀ 300 mls//10 fl oz sour cream

☀ 4 chopped tomatoes     ☀ Chopped parsley – 1 small bunch

## METHOD:

1. Turn your slow cooker onto a low heat then heat up 2 tablespoons of oil in your deepest skillet over a mid to high heat.

2. Add the beef and sear it until it has browned well on every side then transfer onto a plate.

3. Pour the rest of the oil into the skillet then add the onions and fry for 10 minutes.

4. Add the garlic and peppers, frying for 10 minutes more.

5. Stir the flour and spices into the skillet and cook for another 2 minutes before stirring in the tomatoes, beef stock and tomato puree.

6. Simmer then add the mixture into your slow cooker along with the beef.

7. Cover the beef completely with the rest of the stock then cover with the lid.

8. Allow to cook for 6 to 7 hours.

9. Add the sour cream, swirling it well and add the parsley.

10. Serve with brown rice or roast potatoes.

# Best Slow Cooker Soup Recipes

There's never a bad time to have soup, so whether you're looking for a simple supper on a busy week day or whether you need a warming treat at the end of a winter's evening, these slow cooked soup recipes are sure to tick all your boxes. Comforting, delicious and hearty, these crock pot soups are sure to be devoured by the entire family thanks to the wonderful way in which the slow cooker allows the flavors to simmer for hours together for a richer and tastier meal.

Since you'll have prepared all of the ingredients in minutes, the slow cooker does all the hard work for you. Just throw everything into the pot, switch the appliance on and head out of the door to go about your day. When you return home, pop on your pajamas, get a bowl, fill it with soup and enjoy a relaxing meal in front of the fire!

# HAMBURGER SOUP

It may sound strange, but hamburger soup could become your next go-to meal for the whole family to enjoy. It's not only inexpensive, easy and quick to prepare, it's also very satisfying and hearty thanks to the ground beef, carrots, potatoes, diced tomatoes, bell peppers and celery all cooked in a smoky tomato broth.

*Serves four*
*Preparation time – 15 minutes*
*Cooking time – 3 to 8 hours*

## NUTRITION PER PORTION:

KCAL – 391

FAT – 14 G

SATURATES – 5 G

CARBS – 21 G

SUGARS – 8 G

FIBER – 5 G

PROTEIN – 46 G

## INGREDIENTS:

- 450 g//1lb of ground beef
- 3 chopped carrots
- 1 chopped onion
- 3 chopped celery stalks
- 450g// 1lb chopped red potatoes
- 1 chopped green pepper
- 1 ½ litres// 7 cups of beef broth
- 1 can of chopped tomatoes
- 1 can of tomato sauce
- 2 teaspoons of chilli powder
- 2 teaspoons of beef bouillon
- 1 teaspoon of salt
- 1 teaspoon of garlic powder
- 1 teaspoon of ground cumin

- ½ teaspoon of dried parsley
- ½ teaspoon of dried basil
- ½ teaspoon of dried oregano
- 1 tablespoon of apple cider vinegar
- ½ teaspoon of pepper
- 1 tablespoon of brown sugar
- ½ teaspoon of smoked paprika
- 1 tablespoon of mustard
- 2 teaspoons of liquid smoke
- 1 tablespoon of Worcestershire sauce

## METHOD:

1. Brown the beef along with the celery, carrots and onions over a mid to high heat. Meanwhile, prepare the peppers and potatoes.

2. Add the beef and vegetables together with the rest of the ingredients to your slow cooker along with the broth.

3. Cook on a high setting for 3 to 4 hours. Alternative, cook on a low setting for between 6 and 8 hours.

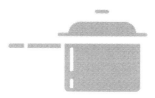

# PEANUT BUTTER AND PUMPKIN CHICKEN SOUP

This easy to cook soup is made with pumpkin puree, coconut milk, delicious spices and peanut butter for a healthy and delicious protein-packed treat. Its warming and unique flavors will appeal to everyone and you can serve it alone or with naan bread and rice for a complete weeknight meal.

*Serves six*
*Preparation time – 10 minutes*
*Cooking time – 3 hours and 10 minutes*

### NUTRITION PER PORTION:
KCAL – 326
FAT – 17.9 G
SATURATES – 5.9 G
CARBS – 14 G
SUGARS – 4.1 G
FIBER – 5.4 G
PROTEIN – 30.3 G

## INGREDIENTS:

- 1 can of coconut milk
- 350 mls//1 1/2 cups of chicken broth
- 1 can of pumpkin puree
- 2 tablespoons of peanut butter
- 1 tablespoon of grated ginger
- ½ teaspoon of cayenne pepper
- 3 minced garlic cloves
- ½ teaspoon of salt
- 700 g//1 1/2lbs of chicken breast without the skin
- 1 diced onion

## METHOD:

1. Add the coconut milk, pumpkin puree, chicken broth, peanut butter, garlic, ginger, salt and cayenne pepper to your slow cooker and mix together until well-combined and smooth.

2. Add the diced onion and chicken breast to the slow cooker.

3. Cover with the lid then cook on a high temperature setting for 3 or 4 hours.

4. Take the chicken out of the cooker and put it on a chopping board.

5. Shred it using forks before adding it back into your slow cooker.

6. Pour the soup onto bowls.

# BEER AND POTATO CHEESE SOUP

This may sound like a strange combination of ingredients, but you're sure to appreciate the unusual flavors that this soup conjures up. It's smooth, creamy and rich enough to satisfy even the hardest to please palate, and when served up with crusty bread it makes a filling and hearty meal for a cold winter's night.

*Serves 6*
*Preparation time – 10 mins*
*Cooking time – 4 hrs*

**NUTRITION PER PORTION:**

KCAL – 466

FAT – 34 G

SATURATES – 21 G

CARBS – 18 G

FIBER – 2 G

PROTEIN – 20 G

## INGREDIENTS:

- 700g//11/2 lbs peeled and chopped potatoes
- 200g//1 cup chopped onions
- 50g//1/3 cup chopped celery stalks
- 2 tablespoons of vegetable oil
- 2 minced garlic cloves
- ½ teaspoon of salt
- ½ teaspoon of dried thyme
- 1 teaspoon of dry mustard
- ¼ teaspoon of black pepper
- ¼ teaspoon of red pepper crushed flakes
- 1 litre//4 cups chicken broth
- 200g//2 cups of grated cheese
- 1 cup of beer

- 16 tablespoons of double cream// heavy cream
- 2 sliced green onions

## METHOD:

1. Put the onion, potatoes, garlic, celery, salt, oil, mustard, pepper flakes, black pepper and thyme into a bowl. Combine well and put into a microwave.
2. Cook in the microwave for 5 minutes.
3. Put the mix into your slow cooker and add the beer and chicken broth.
4. Put on the lid then cook at a low setting for 4-5 hours. Alternatively, cook on a high setting for 3-4 hours.
5. Put the mix into your blender then blend well until smooth.
6. Put the mix back into your slow cooker then stir the cheese until it melts.
7. Stir the cream into the mix and allow to heat for around 5 minutes until warmed through.
8. Sprinkle the green onions over the top then serve.

# TUSCAN LEMON AND WHITE BEAN SOUP

Cozy yet surprisingly light, this warming soup can be served as a satisfying, healthy dinner or as a refreshing springtime lunch. With its Italian influences, it's the ideal choice for the whole family and with its easy-to-prepare recipe, it's perfect for any weekday.

> *Serves four*
> *Preparation time – 10 minutes*
> *Cooking time – 4 hours*

**NUTRITION PER PORTION:**

KCAL – 298

FAT – 9.7 G

SATURATES – 3.6 G

CARBS – 33 G

FIBER – 9 G

PROTEIN – 21 G

## INGREDIENTS:

- 1 ½ litres//6 cups of vegetable or chicken stock
- 100g//½ cup of uncooked quinoa
- 2 chopped carrots
- 1 chopped onion
- 50g//¼ cup of basil pesto
- 4 leaves of sage
- ½ teaspoon of red pepper crushed flakes
- 1 rind of parmesan cheese
- 3 tablespoons of lemon juice
- 1 tablespoon of lemon zest
- Cans of drained cannellini beans
- 200g//2 cups of kale roughly torn
- Grated parmesan cheese to serve

## METHOD:

1. Combine the quinoa, stock, carrots, onion, pepper flakes, pesto and safe in your slow cooker then add the rind of parmesan cheese. Cover the pot then cook at a low setting for around 4 to 5 hours or at a high setting for 2 to 3 hours.

2. Around 1/2 an hour before you serve the soup, stir the lemon zest and juice into the soup along with the beans and kale.

3. Share out the soup into bowls, top with parmesan cheese and then serve with slices of bread.

# TORTILLA CHICKEN SOUP

Simple to prepare and naturally free from gluten, this tortilla chicken soup is delicious and packed with flavor. It's ideal served as an appetizer before a Mexican-inspired dinner or served alone with bread as a nutritious and hearty meal for a winter evening.

*Serves 6 to 8*
*Preparation time – 10 minutes*
*Cooking time – 240 minutes*

**NUTRITION PER PORTION:**

KCAL – 261

FAT – 10.8 G

SATURATES – 2.5 G

CARBS – 24.7 G

SUGARS – 4.4 G

FIBER – 3.8 G

PROTEIN – 18 G

## INGREDIENTS:

- 2 skinless and boneless chicken breasts
- 2 cans of drained and rinsed black beans
- 1 litre//4 cups of chicken stock
- 1 can of chopped tomatoes
- 1 can of drained sweetcorn
- 1 can of green diced chillies
- 4 minced garlic cloves
- 1 dried chilli pepper
- 1 diced onion
- 2 teaspoons of dried cumin
- Fresh wedge of lime
- 1 teaspoon of salt

## METHOD:

1.  Put all of the ingredients into your slow cooker then stir well to combine.

2.  Turn on the slow cooker and cook on a high heat for 3 to 4 hours or on the low heat setting for 6 to 8 hours.

3.  When the chicken has cooked through, take it out of the crock pot and shred with two forks.

4.  Take out the chilli pepper and discard it.

5.  Serve the soup along with freshly squeezed lime juice.

# FRENCH ONION SLOW COOKED SOUP

Onion soup is a French classic and it's especially easy and delicious when cooked in your slow cooker. It takes no time at all to prepare the ingredients and throw them into the crock pot and then you can enjoy the wonderful aromas as you wait to serve up this traditional dish with French bread and cheese.

Serves eight
Preparation time – 20 minutes
Cooking time – 10 hrs

## NUTRITION PER PORTION:

KCAL – 240

FAT – 8.3 G

SATURATES – 4/8 G

CARBS – 33 G

FIBER – 2 G

PROTEIN – 9 G

## INGREDIENTS:

- 1 kg//3 lbs sliced onions
- 3 tablespoons of melted unsalted butter
- 2 teaspoons of brown sugar
- Black pepper and salt
- 6 fresh thyme sprigs
- 1 leaf of bay
- 1 ½ litres//6 cups of beef stock
- 1 sliced French baguette
- 2 teaspoons of sherry vinegar
- 200g//1 cup of Gruyere cheese, shredded

## METHOD:

1. Put the onions into your slow cooker and stir in the brown sugar, melted butter and a teaspoon of salt.

2. Put the bay leaf and thyme sprigs on top then cover with the lid and cook at a high setting for between 8 and 10 hours.

3. Stir the sherry and beef stock into the slow cooker and season well with the pepper and salt.

4. Cover with the lid then cook for another 2 or 3 hours at a high setting.

5. Take the bay leaf and thyme sprigs out of the cooker.

6. Put the slices of French baguette onto an oven tray and put in the oven. Cook until the bread is browned on each side and set to one side.

7. Share out the soup into bowls then top them with the slices of baguette. Sprinkle with the cheese and then put back into the oven for around 2 minutes until the cheese is melted and browned.

8. Serve the soup immediately.

# Best Slow Cooker Dessert Recipes

You're sure to be amazed by all the things you can prepare in a slow cooker. While many people think that they can only make savory dishes in this trusty appliance, in fact desserts are just as easy to make and equally delicious. Whether you love homemade cakes, brownies or fruity desserts, you're going to love them even more when they're cooked in your slow cooker with virtually no effort on your behalf!

It's so easy to make desserts in your slow cooker that even the kids can help with these amazing recipes, and all will taste amazing. There's nothing quite like coming home to freshly cooked sweet treats, so read on to discover wonderful desserts that everyone is sure to love.

# SPICED APPLE SAUCE CAKE

Are there two flavors that complement each other more than cinnamon and apple? Now, you can enjoy both in this wonderful cake that will tantalize your tastebuds. Incredibly easy to prepare, all you need to do is sit back and enjoy the wonderful aromas this cake produces as it cooks in your crock pot.

*Serves 10*
*Preparation time – 15 minutes*
*Cooking time – 2 hours*

**NUTRITION PER PORTION:**
KCAL – 265
FAT – 13 G
SATURATES – 5 G
SUGARS – 23 G
CARBS – 36 G
PROTEIN – 3 G
FIBER – 1 G

## INGREDIENTS:

- 400g//2 cups all-purpose flour
- 11/2 teaspoons of ground ginger
- 1 teaspoon of baking soda
- ¼ teaspoon of ground cloves
- 1 teaspoon of ground cinnamon
- 50g//1/2 cup of unsalted butter
- 1 teaspoon of Kosher salt
- 50g//1/2 cups of sugar
- 2 eggs
- 50g//1/2 cup brown sugar
- 100g//1 cup of apple sauce (unsweetened)
- 1 teaspoon of vanilla extract

## METHOD:

1. Put a 15" piece of baking paper into your slow cooker's bowl, allowing any excess to come up on the sides.

2. Whisk the baking soda, flour, cloves, ginger, salt and cinnamon together in a bowl.

3. Use an electrical mixer to beat together the butter, brown sugar and sugar in a bowl until fluffy and light.

4. Beat the eggs into the mix then add the vanilla and apple sauce. Don't worry if the mix looks curdled as this is normal.

5. Turn the speed of the mixer down to low then add to the egg mix the flour mix gradually, mixing until incorporated.

6. Pour the batter into your slow cooker then cover and cook until set. This takes around 2 – 21/2 hours on a high setting.

7. Remove the cake from the slow cooker by picking up the baking paper carefully. Put the cake onto a cooling rack and allow it to cool down for 15 minutes.

8. Sprinkle icing sugar/confectioners' sugar over the top then serve with cream or ice cream.

# MINTY HOT CHOCOLATE

If you're a fan of peppermint and love hot chocolate, you're certainly going to love this recipe. The ideal way to finish a meal on a winter's day, this hot chocolate will warm you up and make you feel wonderfully comforted and, even better, it's quick and easy to prepare.

*Serves 12*
*Preparation time 5 minutes*
*Cooking time – 2 hours*

**NUTRITION PER PORTION:**
KCAL – 522
FAT – 29 G
SATURATES – 17 G
SUGARS – 52 G
CARBS – 56 G
PROTEIN – 11 G
FIBER – 2 G

## INGREDIENTS:

- 2 litres//8 cups of whole milk
- 2 packs of chocolate chips
- A can of condensed milk
- 60 mls// ¼ cup of vodka or crème de menthe
- 1 tablespoon of vanilla extract
- ¼ teaspoon of salt
- 1 teaspoon of peppermint extract
- Whipped cream
- Candy canes (crushed)

## METHOD:

1. Pour the condensed milk, milk, vodka or crème de menthe, chocolate chips, peppermint extract, salt and vanilla extract into your slow cooker.

2. Put on the lid then cook at a high setting for 2 hours, vigorously whisking partway through so the chocolate can melt more easily.

3. Pour into mugs and squirt the whipped cream onto the top.

4. Sprinkle on the candy canes and serve immediately.

# CHOCOLATE PEANUT BUTTER CAKE

Peanut butter and chocolate go together perfectly and when combined in this tasty, easy to prepare cake, they make the ideal dessert or a sweet treat for any time of the day. An American classic, you're sure to love this recipe and the kids are sure to love it too.

*Serves 10*
*Preparation time – 15 mins*
*Cooking time – 2 hrs*

**NUTRITION PER PORTION:**
KCAL – 607
FAT – 39 G
SATURATES – 13 G
SUGARS – 37 G
CARBS – 57 G
PROTEIN - 13 G
FIBER – 3 G

## INGREDIENTS:

- 1 pack of cake mix (devil's food cake)
- 50g//1/2 cup of melted salted butter
- 250 mls//1 cup water
- 3 eggs
- 2 packs of peanut butter mini cups
- 100g//1 cup of peanut butter
- 3 tablespoons of icing sugar

## METHOD:

1. Mix together the water, cake mix, eggs and butter in a bowl until smooth then stir the peanut butter mini cups into the mix.

2. Spray non-stick spray into your slow cooker and then add the prepared batter mix. Spread it into a smooth layer.

3. Put on the lid, turn the heat setting to high and cook for 2 hours.

4. Take the cake out of the slow cooker.

5. Put the peanut butter into a pan and warm it on a mid to high heat on your stove top, stirring well until it is smooth and melted.

6. Add the icing sugar then whisk well until smooth.

7. Pour this mix over the cake and top with a packet of the peanut butter mini cups.

8. Serve with whipped cream or ice cream.

# CARAMEL BUTTERSCOTCH CAKE

Whether you're keen to make a delicious dessert to serve at the end of a family meal or whether you're just interested in preparing a simple sweet snack to enjoy at any time, this caramel and butterscotch cake can be prepared quickly and easily and cooked in your slow cooker with absolutely no effort on your behalf.

*Serves 4*
*Preparation time – 10 minutes*
*Cooking time – 2 hours*

**NUTRITION PER PORTION:**
KCAL – 806
FAT – 33.3 G
SUGARS – 99 G
CARBS – 123 G
FIBER – 3 G

## INGREDIENTS:

- 1 box of caramel cake mix
- A stick of butter plus 2 tablespoons of butter
- 100 mls//1/2 cup milk
- 1 pack of butterscotch chips
- Caramel sauce to drizzle
- 500mls//1 ¾ cups boiling water

## METHOD:

1. Heat the slow cooker for 10 minutes before starting to make your cake.

2. Set aside a cup of cake mix.

3. Melt the butter and add to the rest of the caramel cake mix in a bowl.

4. Add the milk then stir well until the batter becomes smooth and thick.

5. Pour this prepared batter into your slow cooker and spread with a spoon evenly over the bottom.

6. Open the pack of butterscotch chips then sprinkle them over the cake layer.

7. Put the reserved caramel cake mix into a bowl.

8. Melt 2 tablespoons of butter and add to the cake mix.

9. Pour in the water then stir it well until mixed thoroughly.

10. Mix this mix over the cake inside the slow cooker.

11. Leave for 2 hours to cook. The cake should then have set firmly at the center.

12. Drizzle with caramel sauce and serve with cream or ice cream.

# CHOC CHIP COOKIE BARS

Everyone loves chocolate chip cookies and now you can prepare them in your slow cooker and serve them in handy bars that are ideal for school packed lunches or as an easy snack at any time. Quick and simple to make, these cookie bars are sure to satisfy even the sweetest tooth.

*Serves 10*
*Preparation time – 5 mins*
*Cooking time – 3hrs*

**NUTRITION PER PORTION:**
KCAL – 462
FAT – 10 G
SATURATES – 6 G
SUGARS – 18 G
CARBS – 82 G
FIBER – 3 G

## INGREDIENTS:

- 200g//1 cup melted salted butter
- 400g//2 cups of brown sugar
- 2 eggs
- 3 teaspoons of vanilla extract
- 400g//2 cups of flour (all-purpose//plain)
- ¼ teaspoon of salt
- 200g//1 cup of chocolate chips

## METHOD:

1. Use aluminum foil to line your slow cooker creating a bowl of foil.

2. Mix the brown sugar and melted butter together in a bowl and stir until smooth.

3. Crack the eggs into the bowl along with the vanilla extract then stir until smooth once more.

4. Stir the flour and salt into the bowl and combine the mix well.

5. Pour the batter into the foil lining of the slow cooker.

6. Pour the chocolate chips over the top.

7. Put the slow cooker's lid on and cook at a high setting for 3 hours.

8. Take the cookies out of the cooker using the foil to lift them.

9. Allow to cool for 1 hour then cut and serve.

# SLOW COOKED CHEESECAKE

Cheesecake is one of the best desserts of all time and now you can enjoy this smooth and creamy treat all prepared in your slow cooker. It won't crack, unlike cheesecakes made in your oven, and it involves very little effort on your behalf. There's no way you can mess this recipe up so give it a try!

*Serves 20*
*Preparation time – 10 mins*
*Cooking time – 5hrs*

**NUTRITION PER PORTION:**

KCAL – 278

FAT – 20 G

SATURATES – 11 G

SUGARS – 15 G

CARBS – 20 G

PROTEIN - 4 G

FIBER – 0 G

## INGREDIENTS:

- 12 digestive biscuits//graham crackers, crumbed
- 6 tablespoons of melted butter
- 700g//24oz of cream cheese
- 250g//1 ¼ cups of granulated sugar
- 275g//1 ¼ cups of sour cream
- 5 eggs
- 1 tablespoon of vanilla extract
- 3 tablespoons of flour (all purpose//plain)
- ½ teaspoon of salt

## METHOD:

1. Switch your slow cooker to a low setting and put a piece of baking paper into its bottom. Spray non-stick cooking spray onto the paper.

2. Put the crackers//biscuits into your food processor. Pulse well until crumbs form.

3. Pour the melted butter into the food processor then pulse once more to combine.

4. Put the crumbs in the slow cooker and evenly press them across the bottom to form the base of your cheesecake.

5. Wipe the bowl of your food processor clean then put the sugar and cream cheese into it, pulsing until smooth.

6. Add the eggs, sour cream, salt, vanilla and flour into the food processor then puree until smooth.

7. Pour this filling over your prepared crust.

8. Put the lid on your slow cooker and allow to cook until you can insert a skewer into its center and it will come out clean. This will take between 5 and 7 hours.

9. Make sure any moisture is wiped off the cooker's lid to keep it from dripping onto your cheesecake's top.

10. Put the slow cooker bowl into your refrigerator and allow to chill for 3 hours.

11. Lift the cheesecake completely out of its pot using the paper's edges. Peel back the paper, slice and serve.

# Best Jam And Butter Recipes For Your Slow Cooker

Slow cookers are surprisingly useful for preparing jams and butters. Minimizing the amount of effort it takes to make these tasty spreads, a slow cooker helps you to use up excess fruits in a convenient yet delicious way. Once the slow cooker has done its work, you can simply transfer its contents into a sterilized jar and refrigerate it until you're ready to use it up. It doesn't get any easier than that!

# APPLE ALL DAY BUTTER

It may take all day to prepare this delicious apple butter but we promise it's worth waiting for! Perfect for spreading on toast or even for just eating out of the jar, this slow cooked recipe is the ideal way to use up any leftover apples, and if you have an apple tree in your back yard, it's an even better choice!

> *Servings – 128*
> *Preparation time – 30 minutes*
> *Cooking time – 11 hours*

## NUTRITION PER PORTION:

KCAL – 34

SUGARS – 15 G

CARBS – 9 G

PROTEIN – 0.1 G

## INGREDIENTS:

- 2 ½ kg//5 ½ lbs of peeled and chopped apples
- 800g//4 cups of white sugar
- ¼ teaspoon of ground cloves
- 2 teaspoons of ground cinnamon
- ¼ teaspoon of salt

## METHOD:

1. Put the chopped apples into your slow cooker.

2. Mix the cinnamon with the sugar, salt and cloves in a bowl.

3. Pour this mix over the chopped apples and mix thoroughly.

4. Cover with the lid then cook at a high setting for an hour.

5. Turn the heat down to a low setting then cook for a further 11 hours, occasionally stirring.

6. When the mix is dark brown and thick take off the lid and continue to cook at a low setting for a further hour.

7. Pour the mix into sterilized jars then cover.

8. Freeze or refrigerate.

# RHUBARB AND STRAWBERRY JAM

Whether you're looking for something to spread on your toast in the morning, a tasty filling for a sandwich to go with peanut butter, or a topping for your rice pudding, this rhubarb and strawberry jam will certainly fit the bill and it can all be prepared quickly and easily in your trusty slow cooker.

*Serves 36*
*Preparation time – 15 minutes*
*Cooking time – 7 hours*

## NUTRITION PER PORTION:
KCAL – 35
SUGARS – 9 G
CARBS – 10 G
PROTEIN – 0 G

## INGREDIENTS:

- 1.4kg//3 lbs of fresh strawberries
- 1kg//2lbs of rhubarb
- ½ teaspoon of cinnamon
- 1 cup of sugar

## METHOD:

1. Cut the rhubarb and strawberries into big chunks.

2. Put half the rhubarb and strawberries into the slow cooker then sprinkle half of the sugar over the top.

3. Add the remainder of the rhubarb and strawberries and sprinkle the rest of the sugar over the top.

4. Sprinkle the cinnamon over everything.

5. Switch on the slow cooker to a low setting.

6. Cook for 4 hours then take off the lid, allowing the mix to continue cooking.

7. After cooking for a total of 5 hours, use a potato masher to mash the mixture well.

8. Cook for a further 2 hours.

9. Switch off the slow cooker and allow to cool completely.

10. When cool, transfer into sterilized jars and refrigerate.

# BANANA BUTTER

If you're looking for an unusual and fruity spread that you can enjoy in a plethora of different ways, this banana butter is the ideal choice. You can use it on toast, of course, but it's also wonderful spread on cakes and on meringues too. It couldn't be quicker or simpler to prepare this spread and the whole family are sure to be impressed by its tasty goodness.

> *Serves 8*
> *Preparation time – 5 minutes*
> *Cooking time – 4 hours*

**NUTRITION PER PORTION:**

KCAL – 26.9

FATS – 0.1 G

SATURATES – 0 G

SUGARS – 2.8 G

CARBS – 6.9 G

FIBER – 0.3 G

PROTEIN – 0.1 G

## INGREDIENTS:

- 4 very ripe bananas
- 2 teaspoons of ground cinnamon
- 75g// ¾ cup of Muscovado sugar
- 2 teaspoons of vanilla extract

## METHOD:

1. Slice up the bananas then put them into your slow cooker.

2. Add the remaining ingredients then switch the appliance to a low setting.

3. Cooking for 4 hours.

4. Stir after the first 30 minutes.

5. When the spread is cooked, put in the blender to puree it until smooth.

6. Store inside the refrigerator in a lidded pot. Alternatively, freeze it in separate portions.

# PEACH BUTTER

Who doesn't enjoy the juiciness of ripe peaches? What better way to enjoy their fruity goodness than by turning them into a delicious spread? This easy to prepare recipe is perfect for all kinds of uses including spreading on toast or cake.

*Serves 8*
*Preparation time – 10 minutes*
*Cooking time – 4 hours*

## NUTRITION PER PORTION:
KCAL – 30
FATS – 0 G
SUGARS – 8 G
CARBS – 8 G
PROTEIN – 0 G

## INGREDIENTS:

- 1.4kg//3lbs peaches
- 200g//1 cup sugar
- A squeeze of lemon juice
- 250 mls//1 cup water

## METHOD:

1. Peel the peaches then remove the pit before slicing.

2. Add the sugar, peaches, water and lemon juice to your slow cooker.

3. Cook on a low heat setting for 3 1/2 hours.

4. Puree the mix using a stick immersion blender (take care as the mix is hot).

5. Remove the lid then cook for 30 minutes more until the butter is smooth and thick.

6. Allow to cool.

7. Spoon the peach butter into sterilized jars and refrigerate.

# Unusual Slow Cooker Recipes

Now that we've looked at a wide variety of things you can make in your slow cooker you probably won't be too surprised to learn that there are plenty of other unusual recipes that can be prepared in this way. Here, we take a look at some of the more unique dishes that can be made quickly and conveniently in this handy gadget, freeing up your time while still making wonderfully flavorsome foods!

# CARAMEL APPLES

It couldn't be easier to make caramel apples in a slow cooker, and even better, it's easier to clean the mess this way! The ideal treat for a fall or winter snack, and an absolute essential for Halloween, these sweet treats are sure to please the kids as well as the grown ups!

> *Serves 4*
> *Preparation time – 5 minutes*
> *Cooking time – 1 hour*

## NUTRITION PER PORTION:
KCAL – 304
FATS – 0.4 G
SATURATES – 0.1 G
SUGARS – 73 G
CARBS – 80 G
FIBER – 4.4 G
PROTEIN – 1.8 G

## INGREDIENTS:

- 1 bag of caramels (unwrapped)

- 4 apples

- 2 tablespoons water

## METHOD:

1. Put a liner into the slow cooker.

2. Put a bag of caramels with the wrappers still on into the slow cooker along with the water.

3. Turn the slow cooker onto a high heat setting.

4. Cook until the caramels have begun to melt.

5. Pierce the apples with skewers.

6. Roll the apples into the caramel.

7. Remember to work quickly since caramel will harden quickly.

8. Throw out the liner once you're done.

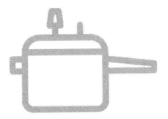

# CHEX MIX

You probably never knew that Chex Mix could be prepared in a slow cooker, but it's surprisingly easy and wonderfully delicious. If you've never tried it before, you'll wonder why you waited so long when you give this recipe a go!

*Serves 12*
*Preparation time – 10 mins*
*Cooking time – 180 mins*

## NUTRITION PER PORTION:

KCAL – 100

FATS – 3 ½ G

SATURATES – 2 G

SUGARS – 0 G

FIBER – 1 G

CARBS – 15 G

PROTEIN – 1 G

## INGREDIENTS:

- 1 box of Chex cereal
- 400g//2 cups pretzels
- 6 tablespoons of melted, hot butter
- 200g//1 cup of peanuts
- 200g//1 cup of Cheerios cereal
- 60mls//1/4 cup of Worcestershire sauce
- 1 tablespoon of salt

## METHOD:

1. Add the pretzels, cereal, peanuts and Cheerios into your slow cooker's bowl.

2. In another bowl, beat together the salt and butter until all of the salt has been fully dissolved.

3. Add the 60mls//1/4 cup of Worcestershire sauce and stir well until combined.

4. Pour the sauce over the mixture of cereals.

5. Toss for 1 minute until the mix is combined evenly.

6. Cover the slow cooker with its lid and cook on a low setting for 3 hours.

7. Stir after 1 hour, after 2 hours and after 2 ½ hours to prevent the mixture from burning.

8. Remove the mixture from the slow cooker.

9. Spread it on parchment paper evenly in a single layer.

10. Allow to cool down.

11. Store inside a well-sealed container or serve immediately.

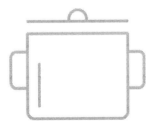

# GREEK YOGURT

Of all the things you probably considered making in your slow cooker, Greek yogurt was probably pretty low on your list! Yet, it's very simple to make using just a handful of ingredients. This is a foolproof recipe, so try it and you're sure to be impressed!

*Serves 12*
*Preparation time – 9 hours*
*Cooking time – 5 hours*

**NUTRITION PER PORTION:**

KCAL – 120

FATS – 5 G

SATURATES – 3 G

SUGARS – 11 G

FIBER – 0 G

CARBS – 12 G

PROTEIN – 8 G

SALT – 0.3 G

## INGREDIENTS:

- 4 ½ liters//1 gallon of whole milk

- 600g//3 cups of powdered milk

- 100g//1/2 cup of plain yogurt that contains active cultures

## METHOD:

1. Pour the milk into the slow cooker then stir in the 600g//3 cups of powdered milk. This will ensure a thick and creamy texture.

2. Switch your slow cooker to a low heat setting then allow the milk to heat to 180 degrees Fahrenheit. This will take about 5 hours.

3. Switch the slow cooker off so the milk begins to slightly cool.

4. When the milk has reached 95 degrees Fahrenheit, take a little milk out of the pot and put it in a bowl with the plain yogurt.

5. Stir the milk and yogurt well together until blended.

6. Pour the mixture into the milk inside the slow cooker.

7. Put the mixture into jars and put inside the oven.

8. Allow the yogurt to remain there for 9 hours. This completes the culture process. Avoid stirring or moving the yogurt.

9. Once the 9 hours is up, take the containers and move them into the fridge.

10. Allow to chill completely before eating.

# OVERNIGHT OATMEAL

There aren't many breakfasts that are quite as comforting when you have to get up early in the winter months than a delicious bowl of toasty hot oatmeal. Just a couple of minutes to prepare this dish the evening before yields a slow cooker full of tasty warm goodness ready for the morning.

*Serves 8*
*Preparation time – 5 minutes*
*Cooking time – 7 hours*

**NUTRITION PER PORTION:**
KCAL – 241
FATS – 12 G
SATURATES – 10 G
SUGARS – 13 G
FIBER – 4 G
CARBS – 32 G
PROTEIN – 5 G

## INGREDIENTS:

- 500g//2 ½ cups diced pears
- 200g//1 cup of oats
- 2 tablespoons of brown sugar
- 75g//1/3 cup of golden raisins
- 3 tablespoons of honey
- ¼ teaspoon of salt
- 2 tablespoons of melted butter
- ¼ teaspoon of cinnamon
- 350 mls//1 ½ cups of milk
- 1/8 teaspoon of ground nutmeg

1. Add a layer of non-stick spray or butter to the slow cooker to coat it.

2. Add the ingredients to the slow cooker.

3. Add boiling water.

4. Stir well then cook on a low heat setting overnight for 7 hours.

# SLOW COOKED LOAF

It's well known that if you want to sell your home, the best way to do it is to cook fresh bread. Now, you can do it the easy way with your slow cooker. It couldn't be simpler to throw the ingredients together and then to just wait for your loaf to rise and cook without any of the stress of making it in the oven in the regular way. This loaf is so simple to make that even beginners can achieve success.

*Serves – Makes one loaf*
*Preparation time – 15 minutes*
*Cooking time – 2 hours*

### NUTRITION PER PORTION:

KCAL – 179

FATS – 1 G

SATURATES – 0 G

SUGARS – 1 G

FIBER – 5 G

CARBS – 32 G

PROTEIN – 8 G

## INGREDIENTS:

- 500g//2 ½ cups of strong white or wholemeal flour
- 1 sachet of dried fast action yeast
- A pinch of sea salt
- 350mls//10 fl oz warm water

## METHOD:

1.  Mix together the salt, yeast and flour in a bowl.

2.  Make a hole in the center.

3.  Pour the water into the hole in the mix.

4.  Mix well together using a spoon or your fingers until the mix becomes a wet, workable, pillowy dough. If necessary, you can add a little more water.

5.  Tip out the dough on a floured surface.

6.  Lead for ten minutes until the dough is elastic and smooth.

7.  Roll the dough until it becomes a tight, large ball.

8.  Put the ball of dough onto baking parchment.

9.  Lift up the dough using the parchment paper into the slow cooker.

10. Put the lid on the slow cooker and turn the heat setting to high.

11. Cook for 2 hours.

12. Take the loaf out of the slow cooker by lifting the parchment paper.

13. You should notice the top is springy and the bottom is crusty.

14. If you would like your bread to have a gold color and crust allow it to cool after taking it out of your slow cooker then put it into an oven for 10 minutes.

# BONUS RECIPES

## Vegan And Vegetarian Slow Cooker Recipes

Although slow cookers are most commonly linked with meat and poultry dishes, it's just as easy to prepare vegetarian and vegan dishes too. In fact, these plant-based meals are just as delicious as any meat based slow cooked dinner thanks to the way that slow cooking allows the flavors to develop fully. Whether you're preparing a meal for a vegetarian friend or family member or whether you're keen to reduce the amount of meat you consume on a daily basis, a slow cooker is the ideal way to achieve your goal. You won't need to slave over a hot stove or spend hours stirring and mixing – all you need to do is chop and prepare a few ingredients and then let your appliance take the strain!

# VEGAN SLOW COOKED RATATOUILLE

One of the most popular plant-based dishes of all is the classic French dish ratatouille. You can serve this slow cooked version as a side dish or as a vegan main meal. This dish can easily be cooked and then frozen to make a simple midweek meal whenever you're too busy to cook from scratch. It delivers 4 of your five a day too, so it's full of nutrients as well as delicious!

*Serves 6*
*Preparation time – 10 minutes*

**NUTRITION PER PORTION:**

KCAL – 162

FATS – 5 G

SATURATES – 1 G

CARBS – 17 G

SUGARS – 16 G

FIBER – 11 G

PROTEIN – 6 G

## INGREDIENTS:

- 2 tablespoons of olive oil
- 2 cloves of garlic
- 1 sliced red onion
- 2 aubergines cut up into pieces measuring 1.5cm
- 3 halved courgettes sliced into pieces of 2cm
- 3 peppers cut up into pieces of 2cm
- 1 tablespoon of tomato puree
- A handful of roughly chopped basil
- 6 chopped ripe tomatoes
- A few sprigs of thyme

☼ 1 can of plum tomatoes

☼ A teaspoon of brown sugar

☼ 1 tablespoon of red wine vinegar

## METHOD:

1. In a skillet, heat up the olive oil then fry the red onion for 8 minutes until translucent.

2. Put the garlic cloves into the skillet then fry for a further 1 minute.

3. Turn up the heat to a medium-high temperature.

4. Add the chopped aubergines then fry for 5 minutes until golden brown.

5. Add the peppers and courgettes to the skillet.

6. Fry for 5 minutes more until the vegetables are slightly soft.

7. Put the fresh tomatoes, tomato puree, canned tomatoes, herbs, sugar, vinegar and salt into the pan and boil.

8. Put all of the cooked ingredients into your slow cooker and turn the temperature to a low setting.

9. Cook for 5 to 6 hours until the sauce is thick.

10. Serve with slices of sourdough bread.

# SPICED VEGAN LENTIL AND ROOT CASSEROLE

This vegan dish isn't just delicious, it's also very hearty and nutritious, supplying a host of vitamins that you need for health and wellness. The lentils add protein while the curry powder adds a touch of exotic flavoring that makes this the ideal winter supper for all the family, whether or not they are vegetarian. Get a good start on your 5 a day with this wonderful and convenient casserole.

*Serves 4*
*Preparation time – 20 minutes*
*Cooking time 5 ½ hours*

## NUTRITION PER PORTION:

KCAL – 333

FATS – 9 G

SATURATES – 1 G

CARBS – 44 G

SUGARS – 13 G

FIBER – 15 G

PROTEIN – 13 G

## INGREDIENTS:

- 2 tablespoons of olive oil
- 3 peeled and sliced carrots
- 1 chopped onion
- 5 peeled and sliced parsnips
- 3 crushed cloves of garlic
- 2 tablespoons of curry powder
- 1 tablespoon of smoked paprika
- 150g//3/4 cup of rinsed red lentils
- 600mls//2 ½ cups of vegan stock
- Lemon juice
- Bay leaves

## METHOD:

1. Turn your slow cooker onto a low heat setting.

2. In a skillet heat up the olive oil then cook the onions for 10 minutes.

3. Add the parsnips and carrots then cook for 10 more minutes until the vegetables are turning golden brown.

4. Add the spices and garlic then cook for another 5 minutes, stirring all the time.

5. If needed, add a little water.

6. Pour all the cooked ingredients from the skillet into your slow cooker.

7. Stir the lentils, bay leaves, seasoning and stock into your slow cooker.

8. Put on the lid then cook at a low setting for 6 hours until the sauce is thick and the veg is tender.

9. Stir lemon juice in to taste.

10. You can then serve with potatoes, rice or bread.

# VEGAN CURRY

Vegetable curry is a classic dish that everyone will enjoy, whether or not they are vegan or vegetarian. However, when you prepare it in the slow cooker you can really enjoy all of the advantages of the simplicity that this handy kitchen appliance brings. Mild and tasty, this is an ideal weeknight dinner and it's sure to satisfy even the hardest to please member of your family.

*Serves 2*
*Preparation time – 10 minutes*
*Cooking time – 6 hours*

**NUTRITION PER PORTION:**

KCAL – 391

FATS – 22 G

SATURATES – 13 G

CARBS – 30 G

SUGARS – 18 G

FIBER – 14 G

PROTEIN – 11 G

## INGREDIENTS:

- 1 can of coconut milk
- 2 teaspoons of vegetarian bouillon powder
- 3 tablespoons of curry paste
- 1 sliced and deseeded red chilli
- 1 tablespoons of ginger, finely chopped
- 3 sliced garlic cloves
- 200g//1 cup of chopped butternut squash
- 1 sliced and deseeded red pepper

☀ A handful of chopped fresh coriander

☀ 160g//3/4 cup of defrosted frozen peas

☀ Juice of 1 lime

## METHOD:

1. Put the curry paste, coconut milk, chilli, bouillon powder, garlic, ginger, aubergine, pepper, and butternut squash into your slow cooker. Stir well.

2. Put the lid onto the pot and cook on a low setting for 6 hours.

3. Stir the defrosted peas and coriander into the mix.

4. Add a squeeze of the lime juice.

5. Serve with wholemeal flatbreads and rice for a delicious Indian-inspired dinner.

# VEGAN MARROW SLOW COOKED WITH TOMATO AND FENNEL

If you're looking for an impressive dish that is warming and hearty enough for winter but also simple enough to prepare any time of the year, this stew is sure to tick your boxes. Flavorsome and easy, you can whip this up quickly whenever you feel the need for a nutritious dinner.

> *Serves 4*
> *Preparation time – 30 minutes*
> *Cooking time – 4 1/2 hours*

## NUTRITION PER PORTION:

KCAL – 459

FATS – 23 G

SATURATES – 8 G

CARBS – 38 G

SUGARS – 14 G

FIBER – 10 G

PROTEIN – 15 G

SALT – 1.3 G

## INGREDIENTS:

- 1 marrow
- 4 tablespoons of olive oil
- 1 sprig of rosemary
- Fennel seeds – a pinch
- Pinch of chilli – dried

- ½ bulb of sliced fennel
- 2 cloves of crushed garlic
- Splash of white wine
- 1 tablespoon of red wine vinegar
- 1 can of chopped tomatoes

☀ 2 tablespoons of capers                    ☀ 1 can of butter beans

## METHOD:

1.  Cut the marrow in half, deseed it and then cut it into large chunks.

2.  Place into a colander and cover with salt.

3.  Allow to drain for 30 minutes so excess water is removed.

4.  Pour the oil into a skillet and heat over a mid to high heat.

5.  Put the fennel seeds and rosemary into the skillet and cook until sizzling.

6.  Put the onion, fennel, and chilli into the skillet.

7.  Allow to cook until the onion begins to color and sweeten.

8.  Add the crushed garlic then cook for 1 minute more, stirring all the time.

9.  Slightly turn the heat up.

10. Pour the marrow into the skillet and cook while stirring for 10 minutes.

11. Use the white wine to deglaze the skillet. Cook until all of the wine has evaporated.

12. Add the red wine vinegar and tomatoes.

13. Stir well until everything is combined.

14. Pour all of the ingredients into your slow cooker and allow to cook at a low heat for 4 hours.

15. Stir the butter beans and capers into the slow cooker and cook for 30 minutes more.

16. Serve with fresh sourdough bread.

# VEGETARIAN LASAGNE

An incredibly popular Italian dish, this vegetable lasagne is not only lower in calories than its meaty alternative but it's also lighter than the classic baked dish. Layered with ratatouille, sliced aubergine and pasta, it also supplies all five of your 5 a day!

*Serves 4*
*Preparation time – 15 minutes*
*Cooking time – 3 hours*

### NUTRITION PER PORTION:
KCAL – 461
FATS – 29 G
SATURATES – 9 G
SUGARS – 14 G
FIBER – 5 G
CARBS – 37 G
PROTEIN – 13 G
SALT – 0.6 G

## INGREDIENTS:

- 1 tablespoon of rapeseed oil
- A deseeded and sliced red pepper
- 2 sliced onions
- 2 chopped garlic cloves
- 2 diced courgettes
- 1 deseeded and sliced yellow pepper
- 1 can of chopped tomatoes
- A handful of chopped fresh basil
- 2 teaspoons of vegetable bouillon

- 1 sliced aubergine (cut across its length)
- 2 tablespoons of tomato puree
- 6 sheets of wholewheat lasagne
- 1 ball of vegetarian mozzarella cheese

## METHOD:

1. Heat up the rapeseed oil inside a non-stick, large pan.
2. Fry the onions and garlic for 5 minutes. Stir frequently.
3. Add the courgettes, peppers and can of tomatoes to the pan.
4. Add the tomato puree, vegetable bouillon and basil. Stir well.
5. Cover then cook for a further 5 minutes.
6. Lay half of the sliced aubergine into the slow cooker's base.
7. Top the aubergine with 3 lasagne sheet.
8. Place 1/3 of the vegetable mixture into the slow cooker.
9. Place the rest of the sliced aubergine on top.
10. Place 3 lasagne sheets over the aubergine.
11. Spoon the rest of the vegetable mix over the top.
12. Place the lid on the slow cooker.
13. Cook at a high setting for 3 hours.
14. Rip up the ball of mozzarella cheese.
15. Scatter it evenly over the lasagne.
16. Cover and allow to settle for 10 minutes until the cheese is melted.
17. Serve with rocket salad and crusty bread for a healthy dinner for all the family.

# SLOW COOKED VEGETARIAN STEW WITH CHEESE DUMPLINGS

The perfect choice for vegetarians on a Fall or Winter weeknight, this stew is comforting, hearty and nutritious. You can also serve it up to vegans without the dumplings.

*Serves 6*
*Preparation time – 20 minutes*
*Cooking time – 6 hours*

## NUTRITION PER PORTION:

KCAL – 554

FATS – 33 G

SATURATES – 17 G

SUGARS – 6 G

FIBER – 13 G

CARBS – 40 G

PROTEIN – 18 G

## INGREDIENTS:

- 2 tablespoons of olive oil
- 3 sliced leeks
- 3 crushed garlic cloves
- 3 tablespoons of flour
- 200g//2 cups of carrots
- 2 sliced courgettes//zucchini

- 1 bay leaf
- 2 cans of cannellini beans
- 400ml//1 ½ cups vegetable stock
- 4 sprigs of thyme
- 200 ml//3/4 cup crème fraiche
- 200g//2 cups of peas

- 1 tablespoon of mustard, wholegrain
- 200g//2 cups spinach

**For the dumplings:**

- 100g//1 cup flour
- 50g//1/2 cup cold butter
- 100g//1 cup cheddar cheese

## METHOD:

1. Turn your slow cooker onto a low setting and in a skillet heat a tablespoon of oil. Fry the chopped carrots until golden, for around 5 minutes, then add them to your slow cooker.

2. Pour the rest of the oil into the skillet then add the leeks. Fry them with a little salt until soft, for around 5 minutes.

3. Add the flour and garlic.

4. Add the vegetarian stock gradually, stirring until there aren't any lumps.

5. Allow to boil.

6. Tip all of the cooked ingredients into your slow cooker.

7. Add the herbs, beans and courgettes//zucchini to the slow cooker.

8. Add water so that all the vegetables are fully covered.

9. Put on the lid and cook for around 4 hours.

10. Meanwhile, prepare the dumplings by putting the butter and flour into a bowl and stirring until distributed evenly. Add the cheese the mix 3 tablespoons of water into the mix using your hands until a sticky, soft dough has formed. Divide the dough into 6 then roll carefully into balls.

11. Put the mustard, crème fraiche, spinach and peas into your slow cooker.

12. Turn the setting up to high.

13. Place the dumplings onto the stew.

14. Put the lid back on and allow to cook for 2 hours.

15. Serve with crusty bread.

# SLOW COOKED VEGETARIAN MACARONI CHEESE

A classic Italian inspired dish that takes you back to your childhood, this vegetarian macaroni cheese is sure to make you feel comforted on even the coldest winter evening.

*Serves 4*
*Preparation time – 15 minutes*
*Cooking time – 1 ½ hours*

### NUTRITION PER PORTION:

KCAL – 666

FAT – 31 G

SATURATES – 19 G

CARBS – 71 G

SUGARS – 9 G

FIBER – 4 G

PROTEIN – 25 G

## INGREDIENTS:

- 350g//3 ½ cups macaroni
- 600mls//2 ½ cups milk
- 50g//1/2 cup butter
- 50g//1/2 cup soft cheese
- 100g//1 cup cheese
- 20g//1/4 cup vegetarian parmesan

## METHOD:

1. Cover the pasta with boiling water then drain.

2. Put all the ingredients into your slow cooker.

3. Stir well.

4. Cover with the lid and cook at a low setting for 1 hour.

5. Stir once more then recover and cook again for 30 minutes.

6. Serve with salad.

# VEGETARIAN PESTO AND RICOTTA MUSHROOMS

If you're looking for an unusual and impressive dish to serve up to your vegetarian friends at a dinner party, this Italian-inspired slow cooker dish is sure to tick your boxes. The mushrooms add a little more bite while the pesto adds plenty of mouthwatering flavor.

Serves 4
Preparation time – 15 minutes
Cooking time – 9 hours

**NUTRITION PER PORTION:**

KCAL – 400

FATS – 34 G

SATURATES – 12 G

CARBS – 2 G

SUGARS – 0 G

FIBER – 1 G

PROTEIN – 19 G

## INGREDIENTS:

- 5 tablespoons of olive oil
- 1 tub of ricotta cheese
- 16 chestnut mushrooms
- 2 tablespoons of green pesto
- 25g//1/4 cup grated vegetarian parmesan
- 2 chopped garlic cloves

## METHOD:

1. Trim the stalks of the mushrooms so that they are level with the caps then put them into the slow cooker with the round side downwards.

2. Mix the garlic, pesto and ricotta together.

3. Spoon the mix into the prepared mushrooms.

4. Sprinkle the vegetarian parmesan cheese over the top.

5. Drizzle the oil over the mushrooms.

6. Turn the slow cooker to a low heat and cook for 9 hours.

7. Serve with salad and crusty bread.

# MAKING THE MOST OF YOUR SLOW COOKER

As you can see from the great variety of recipes that we've brought to you in this cookbook, there's an enormous range of dishes and treats that can be made in your slow cooker. Many people think that this kitchen appliance is only useful for stews or casseroles, and while these dishes work well in a slow cooker, the fact is that you aren't restricted only to these simple meals when you invest in this gadget.

Now that you have this recipe book to hand, you'll be able to make the most of your trusty new appliance. You'll soon be whipping up delicious entrees, spectacular appetizers and tasty desserts, not to mention jams and spreads, yogurt, oatmeal and bread! You won't be able to wait to show off your newly acquired slow cooking skills, so whether you're making something special for a dinner party, preparing treats for children's snacks or making a showstopping dessert that's certain to satisfy the sweetest tooth, your slow cooker is at hand ready to make things easier. Never again will you need to slave over that hot stove after a long day at the office – you'll be ready to prep and go. On your return, you'll be welcomed back by the gorgeous aroma of cooking and your dinner will be all ready to bring to the table.

We hope that you enjoy trying out these exciting and varied recipes that are sure to delight you and impress your friends and family. Indeed, you're sure to discover that your new slow cooker is so versatile that you'll wonder how you ever managed without one!

Printed by Amazon Italia Logistica S.r.l.
Torrazza Piemonte (TO), Italy

16853215R00064